NEW SCOTTISH POETRY

Dreams

for the

Seasons

8d

8d Press
Dunfermline
Fife
Scotland
www.8dpress.co.uk

Designed by 8d Press
Printed in Dunfermline by Printing
Services Ltd.

ISBN: 978-0-9935424-4-2

Introduction

In these uncertain times, when the world seems to have gone mad, when we're inundated each day with bad news — whether it be the war in the Ukraine, the disgusting profiteering by the gas and oil companies, the circus that is UK politics, the cost of living crisis or the scary potential re-emergence of the Covid-19 virus, nothing calms and soothes our ragged souls more than the sweetness of poetry.

In *Dreams for the Seasons,* three local writers wrap us in a soft blanket of poetry and the world seems right again.

Poetry heals, poetry soothes, poetry takes us away from our everyday, but also places us firmly in the 'now', reminding us that we are human, we are vulnerable, we are imperfect but we are strong. And we will survive.

We hope you enjoy our little book of poetry *Dreams for the Seasons,* and that you take some time out for yourself every day to reconnect with the language of poetry.

8d Press — Fife, Scotland, November 2022.

Our Poets

E E Benson

Erica Benson is a conservation and environmental scientist. She has a PhD in Marine Biology and has regularly published non-fiction throughout her academic career. Her creative works include a poetry contribution to *LUCENT*, published by 8d Press. She has had several of her haiku pieces read by Poetry Pea and published in the British Haiku Society's journal *Blithe Spirit* and its 2021 anthology.

She is currently writing short eco-stories, poetry and haiku and is working on a compilation of Scottish Island haibun.

Originally from the Yorkshire Dales, Erica has lived in Scotland for over 30 years. She lives in Fife and enjoys exploring Scotland's natural places and watching the wildlife that lives there.

She writes to explore her relationship with the natural world.

Wild Rhythms

Greylag Geese

dreich nights and mornings
greylags honk honk their flybys
October's sound-track

skeins of Vane Farm geese
shift in sky-blue formation
turning the seasons

fair cirrus ice clouds
criss-crossed by visitors' vees
in search of safe ground

a moonlight vixen
flicks fear through flocks of feathers
they're away again...

Grey Seals

Tentsmuir's wailing seals
hauled up for Autumn birthing
seek out safe spaces

among wind chilled rocks
lines of soft blubber boulders
warm the Isle of May

salt waves spit and spray
the grey sea folk's new-born pups
white wide-eyed selkies

watch clouds of pale knots
perform their dazzling sky dance
moving all as one

Redwings & Rowans

expectant rowans
wait for thrushes in the cold
flocks gather by night

redwing eyes perceive
red against the last green leaves
fleshy berry bribes

Icelandic migrants
gorge on scarlet Scottish fruits
life disseminates

redwings are long gone
rowan's winter genes are spread
staining snow blood red

***

Bulrush Magic

Bulrush staffs once held
the magic of Grandmothers

In their golden olden days
They were displayed high and dry
In dark green stoneware
On sacred sideboard altars

DON'T TOUCH!
Front rooms entered ONLY
At CHRISTMAS on RED LETTER DAYS
and AFTER CHAPEL SUNDAYS

Years ago ...
Fidgeting on the prickly horsehair settee
Aunty's MacAssars are no defence
Itching for dinnertime

From their polished perch
The sad bulrushes see everything
Captives of dried flower arranging fads
They have a dark empathic gaze

Like me they're stranded
We're fishes out of water
Taking pity the magic velvet wands
charm my great escape

From my scratchy seat
Into the mirage world below
Of Grandma's threadbare
Oriental carpet

Lions guard the oasis gates
Of a marbled Moorish palace
Where lotus flowers float dreams
In pools of Lapis Lazuli

Balustrades of incensed jasmine
Weave through cypress groves
Along the sparkling waterways
pomegranates grow

Shimmering peacocks scream
In exotic fountain gardens
Luscious fruits ripe to pick
Hang in their filigree orangeries

DANGER!
High winds whip up a sandstorm
SAVED! By a gracious camel
Who takes me on his back

We trek together
For miles and miles and miles
Through drifting desert dunes
Like Lawrence of Arabia

We sleep under the stars
For a thousand and one nights
Coffee crescent moons wax and wane
In the carpet's Black Magic Chocolate sky

'DINNER'S READY LOVE'
Said Grandma
'Where've you been dear?'
'To Arabia and back on a camel'

'How nice,' she said
'NOW WASH YOUR HANDS
'Hope the weather was good
Such a long way to go
You'll be hungry love'

'Yes' I said …
Stepping into the blue and white
Dreamscape of my Sunday dinner
Willow Pattern plate

***

Snow Words

*There are more words for snow in Scots
than in any other language.*

***

tread gently ...
through a soft flindrikin
lightest of all the
snows

an orange tip butterfly
chrysalis hangs by a frosted
silver thread

straight-trotting
roe deer tracks swerve
into a blin-drift

a magnetic mousing fox
jumps! blood spots
... on snow

tread softly ...

laid out on an icy path
the snaw ghaist
of a shrew

flaggies gather
around street lights
like ermine moths

snawmen
linger longer
in the still cold sun

a thow wind
reveals the dog fox's
skeleton

tread quietly ...

inside the
snow globe magic
of a swirling feefle forest

under the bark
of an ancient oak
a tree creeper sleeps

ice stars twinkle in the glister
of a twilight wood
a robin sings

shy roe deer
nibble frosted kale
in a new day's scowtherin

tread carefully ...

a strong jeelit wind
spitters snaw-rashed skin
red raw

flukra flakes
clump on sodden
woollen mittens

frozen white breath
is snatched away
by a blustery snell

green fringed
snow drops peep
through glistening skimmerin

tread lightly ...

leave no trace
while walking East Lomond's
wild snaw breist

deep in a murg
covering Benarty Hill
a gentle shivering giant sleeps

chattering winter words
for ice and snow
and wreaths

tread lightly
through a soft flindrikin
gentlest of all the snows

***

Glossary

Blin-drift snow drift.
Feefle swirling snow.
Flindrikin a very light snow shower.
Flaggies large snowflakes.
Flukra a large snowflake.
Glister a thin covering of snow or ice.
Jeelit absolutely (bloody) freezing.
Murg heavy fall of snow.
Scowtherin a sprinkling of newly fallen.
Skimmerin a light sprinkle of powdery snow.
Snaw Snow.
Snaw breist a snow covered hill.
Snaw ghaist ghostly apparition seen in the snow.
Snawman/men snowman/men.
Snell bitterly cold.
Spitter(s) small wind-driven snowflake(s).
Thow wind a thawing wind breaking a long frost.
Wreaths snow drifts.
Source: Glasgow University Snow | Historical Thesaurus of Scots (scotsthesaurus.org)

Poet's note for reference: Red foxes in the Northern Hemisphere use their 'extra-sensory' perception of the Earth's magnetic field to sense and capture prey hidden deep in the snow.

Bill Devlin

Bill Devlin is Fife writer. He lives with his wife in Windygates, close to Leven, on the Fife coast.

He studied Psychology and English at the University of Dundee and has taught Creative Writing at the Workers' Educational Association.

He is currently studying the art of memoir writing in Dundee, while working on his own memoir project which he hopes to complete in 2023, all being well.

The Earl and the Poacher

This night against the current of the river
Cusped moon, waning to crescent sliver
A poacher anchors, plaid, faded and worn
Stone-scuffed, brogues stamping their scorn
On a bed of ochre, smudged and sullen clay
A mooring of willows at the cold end of a winter day
Lifting his gaze, he tracks with weather eye
The slink and arch of a sleek, brown otter
Small river bats, white moths as they flicker by
Moor-hens bobbing, eddying in the icy water
The river seeks refuge between roots of sycamores
Past blackened, branches of scorched broom and gorse
Night treads, a fieldmouse, scurrying on fronds of fern
Searching the shadows with neat, twist, step and turn
Snell wind bites beneath a mauve-coloured sky
Senses prickle, prod the darkness, linger and pry;

Rough head framed against the half-light and worn
Winces at a weasel's screech in stubbled fields of corn
Patterns of gypsies and travellers strewn, arrange
Twigs and branches, portents, oblique, strange
Mottled before the trees; he hirples and swears
Blows the fire to a glow and with a sharp knife prepares
A stumped turnip, some berries, a still writhing trout
Gutting and cleaning, his deft business about
A glistening frost spreading, sparse on the starred moss
The moon in relief, a breast and a bruise
Curlews still in the spiky, rimed grass, cower
A dog fox lopes, canny in the gloaming hour
Spent, slender, russet, gone to ground
Hackles bristling, at the cold scent of the hound
In the Lomond hills snow cushions the slopes, sheep lean

In the shelter of twisted larches, witching, black and green
And at the white cottage where he comforts his bones
Time slips its thin blade between mortar and stone
Winter blue-tits feed, a high, shrill whistle
Frosty silver birch branches, glister and rustle
Bounty and graith lodged, boarded; sheltered now
  magpie clipes, fierce on the topmost bough
Morning's routines return, comforting and familiar
Fresh bread baking in the co-op store
Streets alive with the shouts of weans
The rattle of feet in the closes and lanes
Ridding himself of his drab, working costume
  stretches down in the shelter of his room
Mary's sleeps, her red hair tied
With a clasped, tortoise-shell comb

Dwelling a moment with tenderness and pride
The hollow of her shoulder, welcoming home
Treasured face, older, kinder, lined, blessed
Shifting slightly, leaning, rhythming, at rest
The poacher paints a memory, forty years ago
A winsome, young, lass in a dress as white as snow
As the new day wakes, creaks and arranges
The winter sun rises and the light subtly changes
To love, cherish to have and to hold
He smiles at the sweet jest, the tragedy of becoming old.
The wall clock ticks, the hour comes round again
Morning calls for a last, wersch round of single grain
As the liquid hits, and the fire bites
I envy the poacher who has prospered tonight
She lays beside him, breath sweet as lemon and thyme,
And in the bleak of this castle, I wish she were mine

***

When Catholics Get the Blues

Sleepless; dawn comes
Old lovers; separate rooms
Cracked sink, deprivation
Strong drink, double rations
Razor trips, skelves like corn flies
Into shaving foam, practised lies
Random thoughts, too close to home
Ticking of the metronome
Rhythm method; mind control
Slowing down and growing old
Nurse that precious sense of sin
Blood brothers, kith and kin
Change your spots, cast your skin
Stick with it through thick and thin
Front page, evening news
Worn out, thin excuse
Your life, you choose
When Catholics Get the Blues

Deaf ears, dread eyes
Telling blows, telling lies
Home truths, far cries
Dark before sunrise
Time slots; hangovers
Close shaves; beautiful losers
Blind drunk, fear of God
Homeless, poor sod
Headaches and shock waves
Treading on hidden graves
Politics, familiar ruse
Slack conduct; loose screws
Clean shirt, dress shoes
Sunday best, fading bruise
Hard assed, church pews
When Catholics Get the Blues
Yew trees and burial mounds
Ropey logic, sufficient grounds
Lucid dreams, moveable feasts
Fairground magic, honest priests

Muttered prayers, offerings made
Dulled protests, honed blades
Stark branches, copper leaves
Smokers cough, can't breathe
Cheap scent, deep grief
Scars, wounds beneath
Headlines, same old
Bit actor, cameo role
Locks, keys, mysteries, clues
short time, smouldering fuse
Treated like refuse
always something there to lose
when Catholics Get the Blues

***

My Old Friend

It's Christmas Eve, I'm wide awake
The fire settles and embers warm the grate
Be patient; he'll be here she laughs
You know all good things come to those wait
I nod and agree but uneasily sense
Something creeping quietly outside
Scraping stealthily under the fence
Disturbing the hallowed night
I start, staring panicked towards the door
Wincing, out of breath
What's keeping him so long I ask her
I'm worried half to death

A tawny owl wings by, I hear its shriek
A darker silhouette deepens the gloom
Field voles scatter, the wind is bleak
A rustle of cold air creeps round the room
It won't be long, he's getting close
Mind you stay awake
And try and behave when he does arrive
Be civil for once, for heaven's sake!

Times when we woke to the sight, of snow
Clouds furling over our croft in the north
Badgers and foxes, scurrying below
Imprints of hoofs on the hard-rimed earth
He's just next door, I hear her say
They've been waiting too
He'll soon be here, don't lie and mope
Let's find ourselves something useful to do

A crossword solved before the fire
A tinselled silver frost of
Poems and rhymes plucked from mind
From shared, secret caves like ghosts
I'm tired I said, it's getting late
I want to close my eyes and rest
Hush now you've waited up till now
And he is a rather special guest

Strands of tinsel swathe the walls
A silver shawl of memories
Echo beneath the striking clock,

The green and red of a Christmas frieze
He's here she smiles, I'll let him in,
You've waited far too long
He's ready and he remembers both you and I
From the days that we were young

The room and its confines disappear
Footsteps steal over the creaking floor
I can't hear the voice now but I know she's near
Safe beneath her serious gaze
In this last colder month and the beginning of days
I remember who I have been waiting for
And step lissomly through the welcoming door
At last my friend is here

***

Robert Ferguson

Robert Ferguson is a novelist, poet, musician and songwriter. He lives in Alloa, Clackmannanshire, with his wife, Lorna.

He's a father and grandfather, and a passionate animal lover and vegetarian.

He writes short stories ~~larly and he's a strong advocate of personal development, a theme which makes its way into his stories often.

His second novel *Red Lentil Soup*, a psychological thriller, is out on 30th November, and will be available at Waterstones, W.H Smiths and Hive.co.uk

Find him on Facebook at robertmackie.ferguson.5

Alexei Petrenko's forgotten letter

Where are you, young man?
Did you forget to send Santa a letter?

There is no present under the tree
With your name on it, I can see
Did mum or dad forget to say
That I would arrive on Christmas day?

Goodness me, it's only once a year
en me and my reindeer traditionally appear
And here you sleep and dream because,
You've gone and forgotten Santa Clause

ere are mince pies, shortbread and sherry
ur new mother invited me to make merry
But why forget this special day?
That's the reason I'm here today

But wait... are you the boy that fled from war?
Who doesn't believe in me anymore?
Suffering stress, trauma and pain
Efforts to improve, but in vain

That on the streets of Bucha, where much blood was spille
A place where your own parents were killed
Shot before your eyes, then they hit the ground
In a village where much more dead were found

Escaping on a cycle down a tree-lined street
Shot in the hand and twice in the feet
reaching the house finding your sister shot
lifeless and listless alone in her cot

A priest cleaned your wounds and helped you escape
From murders, torture, beatings and rape
An orphaned boy stepping into the unknown
Exploring yourself and being alone

Adopted by people in a far-off land
Your future life is not what you planned
Learning a language to your disdain
And coping with midges and continual rain
Empty and surviving with your loss
Your family buried under a cossack cross
But remember me, *Did Moroz* (Father Frost)
The Ukrainian Santa you have lost

But you will find once you open
Your concealed heart that war has broken
Qualities with love and resources
Predominant passion and affectionate forces

Accept my hands upon your head
Reminding you of what's been said...
Not for war with all its flaws
but reminding you of Santa Clause!

***

Rabbie Burns invented snow

Icy water, slush and sleet
Drove market traders off the street
But, not one of them would likely know
It was Rabbie Burns who invented snow

Ploughing his field with reindeer and sledge
While knocking off snow from the top of a hedge
Covering a moose and her bairns, you know
They knew it was Rabbie Burns who invented snow

When the grey mare meg lost her tail
In blustery weather, she did prevail
Believing her severed tail would grow
She knew it was Rabbie Burns who invented snow

The devil and witches were dancing on ice
Skating with voles, rats and mice
But even these beasties living down low
Knew it was Rabbie Burns who invented snow

If auld acquaintances are not brought to mind
And lesser beings disinclined
A secret trust, which we must bestow
Knowing Rabbie Burns invented snow

When Christmas choirs are joyfully singing
And jingle bell players tunefully ringing
There is something they say that we all must know
That it was Rabbie Burns who invented snow.

***

The Christmas truce at the hotel bin

I see you, Mr Wildcat, hiding amongst the bracken
Your mottled fur and black-tipped tail all but find you..
but what do you see in your stare?
Is it a wee beastie fraught and scared?
And here you are; creeping, sneaking slowly with purpc
to pounce and take its poor life!
Remember, he too, struggles in the onslaught of the win
An ordeal with many challenges of starvation and fami
But look around you, forget the prey
There's a world of nature here at play
other beasts are snooping, watching the scene
biding their time, waiting patiently.

A group of animals are lurking here; hiding, watchin
sniffing the air
concealed in the woodland and under parked cars
they see a wealth of food strewn over the ground

a festive feast with nutrition abound
with thanks to the cleverest carrion crows
for providing such a celebration

umber, broccoli, asparagus and peas colour the
snow
hotel bin has been scattered and ransacked of
human scraps
Pies and potatoes, chicken and beef
Pumpkins, fruitcakes and cabbage leaf
e is more than enough for all of the beasts of
the forest
Dinner for everyone

s call a truce", a red fox said, howling aloud
ing from the thicket and divulging his head

"There is food for all types of tastes
Every scrap with nothing to waste
l be merry, rejoice and survive; make friends
of your enemy
And await our friends to arrive."

49

The animals ate side by side, forgetting the chill and
the scary times
Kill or be killed, passing them by
The wildcat would grimace and swallow his pride
To break down barriers and cross the divide
The rabbit was his friend for one day only
A glorious concept and wintery story

***

8d Press

8d Press is a small, independent publishing house, based in Dunfermline, Fife, Scotland.

We publish limited edition hardbacks, paperbacks and artisan chapbooks, all lovingly produced in the Heritage Quarter of Dunfermline, Fife.

We adhere to the adage 'small is beautiful' and we celebrate 'local' in every sense.

Our beautiful books are not mass-produced. We used sustainable papers and materials, and work only with local artisans to help bring our books and their stories to life.

Our writers are Scottish by birth or immigration, our networks are local and our Press is proud to be small, local and artisan by design.

Visit us at:

www.8dpress.co.uk

Support Scottish Literature

You can support Scottish Literature in the following ways: —

By buying our books from any independent bookseller in Scotland or the UK. If the bookseller of your choice doesn't stock our books you can give them our ISBNs and they will order it for you.

By shopping for our books online through our 8d Press website — www.8dpress.co.uk

By sharing our news & inviting others to buy our books

By subscribing to our newsletter on our website

By following us on social media

By telling your friends about 8d Press

By considering becoming a subscriber — you will find more information is available on options on our website

By supporting your local independent bookseller

8d

8d Press titles

LUCENT — An Ode to Nan Shepherd's The Living Mountain — NEW SCOTTISH WRITING: FICTION: an anthology of twenty-two women writers (hardback): ISBN: 978-0-9935424-8-0

DREAMS FOR THE SEASONS — NEW SCOTTISH POETRY — an anthology of three Scottish poets (paperback): ISBN: 978-0-9935424-4-2

ALONE — journeys inside the solo life — with a foreword by Queen of Crime, Val McDermid: FICTION: an anthology of eight Scottish writers (paperback): ISBN: 978-0-9935424-7-3

105/1000
January 2023
Fife, Scotland